MINI MYTHS
TALES FROM ANCIENT GREECE

HEROIC
HEROES

Michael DeMocker

PURPLE TOAD
PUBLISHING

P.O. Box 631
Kennett Square, Pennsylvania 19348
www.purpletoadpublishing.com

Printing
1   2   3   4   5   6   7   8   9

Fabulous Fables
Heroic Heroes
The Labors of Hercules
Mythical Monsters
Tantalizing Tales

Publisher's Cataloging-in-Publication Data
DeMocker, Michael
  Heroic Heroes / Michael DeMocker
    p. cm.—(Mini myths of Ancient Greece)
      Includes bibliographic references and index.
      ISBN: 978-1-62469-052-5 (library bound)
      1. Mythology, Greek – Juvenile literature.   I. Title.
      BL783 2013
      398.2093802—dc23
                                                      2013936501

eBook ISBN: 9781624690532

ABOUT THE AUTHOR: Despite being a dashingly handsome, globe-trotting, award-winning photojournalist and travel writer based in New Orleans, Michael DeMocker is, in truth, really quite dull, a terrible dancer, and a frequent source of embarrassment to his wife, son and three dogs.

PUBLISHER'S NOTE: The mythology in this book has been researched in depth, and to the best of our knowledge is correct. Although every measure is taken to give an accurate account, Purple Toad Publishing makes no warranty of the accuracy of the information and is not liable for damages caused by inaccuracies.

Printed by Lake Book Manufacturing, Chicago, IL

CONTENTS

INTRODUCTION

Many, many years ago, long before your grandparents' grandparents were born, the ancient Greeks worshiped the Olympian gods— the most powerful being the brothers Zeus, Poseidon, and Hades.

To honor the gods, men went on heroic adventures battling terrible monsters, saving distressed damsels, and becoming legends that live forever in the stories of mankind.

And the greatest of these heroes was Hercules, son of Zeus.

Hercules was famous for his Twelve Labors, a dozen of the nastiest, deadliest chores ever completed. Everyone agrees; he was the greatest Greek . . .

STOP RIGHT THERE!

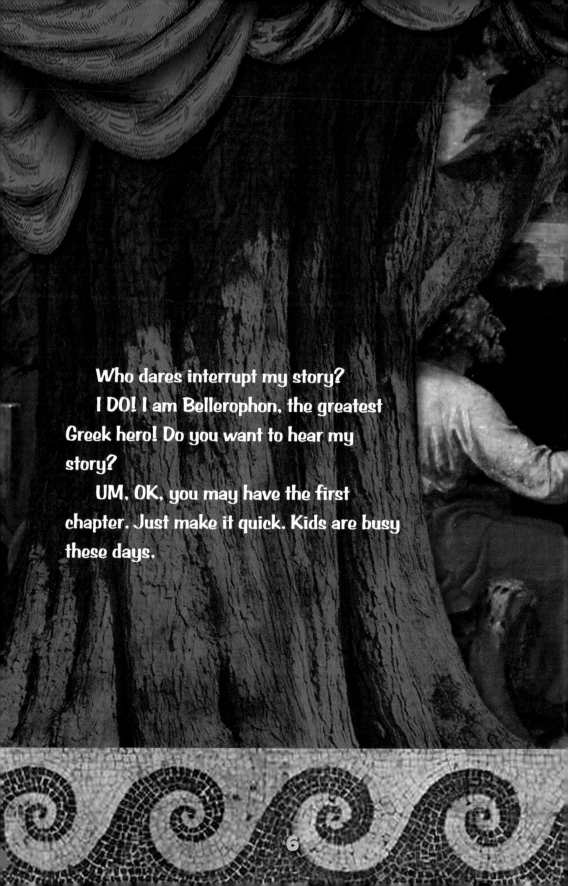

Who dares interrupt my story?

I DO! I am Bellerophon, the greatest Greek hero! Do you want to hear my story?

UM, OK, you may have the first chapter. Just make it quick. Kids are busy these days.

Hello, kids! My name is Bellerophon. Do not listen to the narrator of this book. He is crazy to say Hercules was the greatest of all Greek heroes.

My father is the sea god, Poseidon. I tamed the famous wild, flying horse, Pegasus, after being given a golden bridle by the goddess, Athena.

I know what you're thinking. That other "hero," Perseus, tamed Pegasus. LIES! It was I! Poets gave credit to Perseus centuries later.

After being falsely accused of trying to steal the wife of King Proteus, I was sent to Lycia, which is in modern-day Turkey. There, I had to fight a terrible monster called the Chimaera, a nasty, man-eating beast!

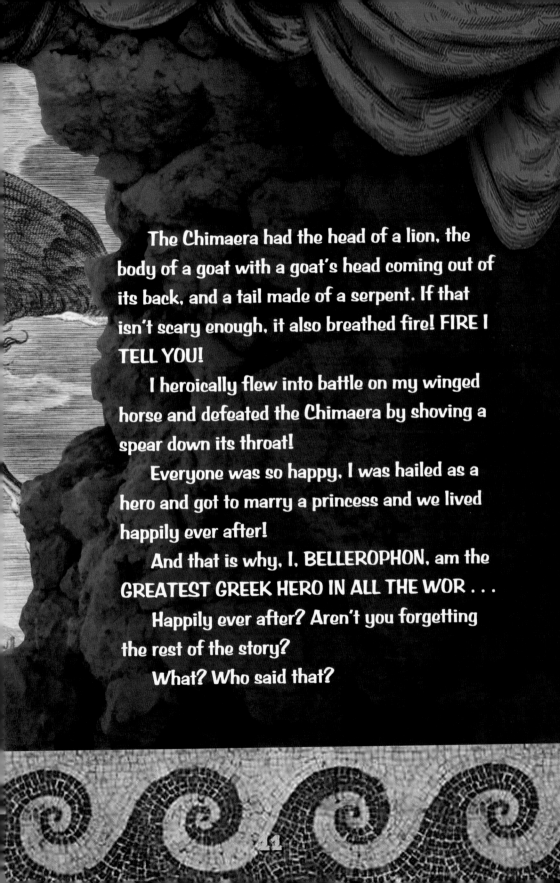

The Chimaera had the head of a lion, the body of a goat with a goat's head coming out of its back, and a tail made of a serpent. If that isn't scary enough, it also breathed fire! FIRE I TELL YOU!

I heroically flew into battle on my winged horse and defeated the Chimaera by shoving a spear down its throat!

Everyone was so happy, I was hailed as a hero and got to marry a princess and we lived happily ever after!

And that is why, I, BELLEROPHON, am the GREATEST GREEK HERO IN ALL THE WOR . . .

Happily ever after? Aren't you forgetting the rest of the story?

What? Who said that?

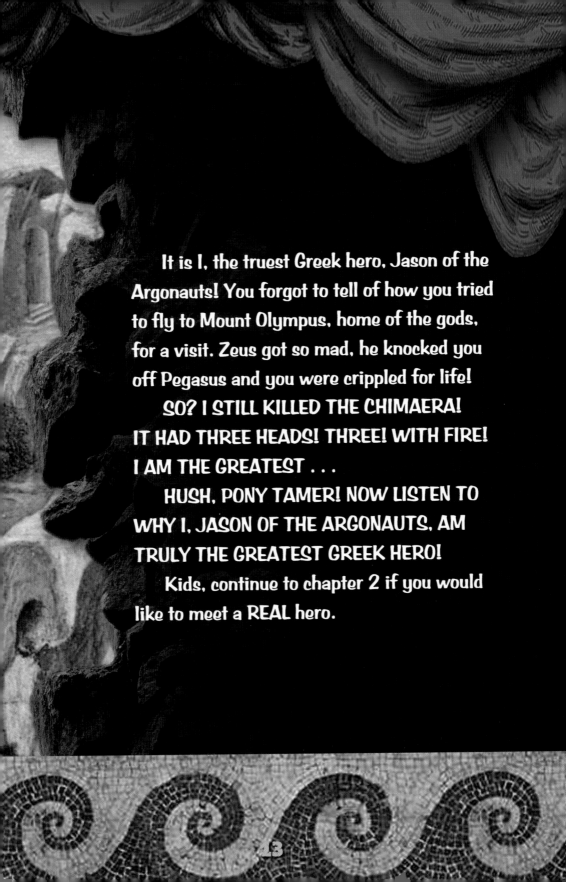

It is I, the truest Greek hero, Jason of the Argonauts! You forgot to tell of how you tried to fly to Mount Olympus, home of the gods, for a visit. Zeus got so mad, he knocked you off Pegasus and you were crippled for life!

SO? I STILL KILLED THE CHIMAERA! IT HAD THREE HEADS! THREE! WITH FIRE! I AM THE GREATEST . . .

HUSH, PONY TAMER! NOW LISTEN TO WHY I, JASON OF THE ARGONAUTS, AM TRULY THE GREATEST GREEK HERO!

Kids, continue to chapter 2 if you would like to meet a REAL hero.

I, Jason, was born a prince, but my evil uncle, Pelias, stole my crown when I was a baby.

WHO STEALS CROWNS FROM BABIES?

I was banished and raised by a magical half-man, half-horse creature called a centaur.

When I grew into a strong young man, Pelias said I could have my kingdom back if I completed an impossible mission—to get the Golden Fleece, a shimmering, wooly skin of a magic ram!

Since the Golden Fleece was hidden far away, and guarded by a horrible serpent monster, my uncle figured I would never return.

HA! He was in for a surprise!

I set sail on a ship called the *Argo* with a group of heroes called the Argonauts. We braved vicious flying bird witches called harpies, sailed between huge rocks that smash together to squish ships, and finally made it to the land of Colchis.

In the kingdom, we got help from the daughter of the king, a magical girl named Medea, who fell in love with me (of course!).

Medea, the musician Orpheus, and I journeyed to the Tree at the End of the World. Sure enough, there was a nasty serpent coiled around the tree, guarding the Golden Fleece.

Medea told Orpheus to play a sweet song on his lyre while she sang a sleeping spell. The serpent fell asleep and flopped onto the ground, and then I heroically captured the Golden Fleece and . . .

WAIT A MINUTE! YOUR GIRLFRIEND DEFEATED THE DRAGON?

. . . Yes, but I got the fleece!

BOO! You're not a hero! You went on a cruise and found a magic sweater. Medea, Orpheus, and the Argonauts did all the hard work!

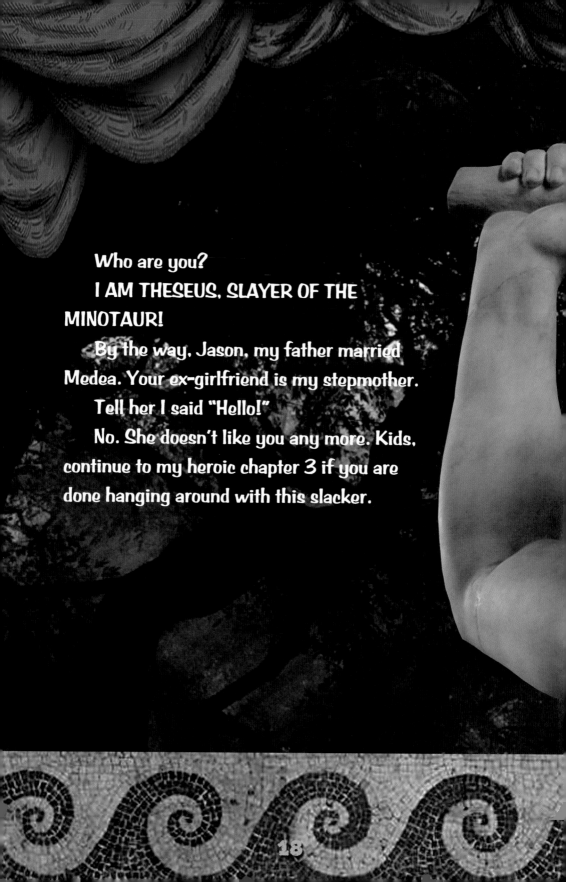

Who are you?

I AM THESEUS, SLAYER OF THE MINOTAUR!

By the way, Jason, my father married Medea. Your ex-girlfriend is my stepmother.

Tell her I said "Hello!"

No. She doesn't like you any more. Kids, continue to my heroic chapter 3 if you are done hanging around with this slacker.

First, let me say that unlike other heroes, I am mortal with no divine blood in me, so that makes my feats extraordinary.

I am the son of King Aegeus of Athens. I grew up wrestling bears for fun and ripping up trees with my powerful arms. I wanted to battle monsters, fight crime, and prove myself worthy of being king.

There was a mean king named Minos who lived on the island of Crete. Because his son died in Athens, he ordered that every nine years, seven boys and seven girls from Athens be sacrificed to a monster called the Minotaur—a huge bull-headed beast that lived inside a giant maze called a labyrinth.

I heroically volunteered to be one of the seven boys. When I got to Crete, the king's daughter, Ariadne, fell in love with me.

Ariadne gave me a golden string to help me find my way out of the maze. I had a long and nasty fight with the giant Minotaur, but in the end I killed it and saved the boys and girls and became king of Athens! Hurray for me!

BOOOORING! Wow! You killed a cow! What a hero!

Hey, I also killed a man with a big club and another who liked to stretch people and cut off their feet!

ZZZZZ. Wake me when you are finished. By the way, Theseus, there's a rumor going around that your father is actually Poseidon, god of the sea.

Not true! Lies! No way!

Hey, kids, leave this cow-slaying "hero" and read about me in chapter 4, for I AM PERSEUS!

CHAPTER FOUR
PERSEUS

I, Perseus, am the half-brother of Hercules. The god, Zeus, is my father, and my mother is Princess Danae. My grandfather is King Acrisius of Argo. He was so scared of me that when I was a baby, he stuffed me and my mother in a box and threw us into the sea.

WHO BOXES UP THEIR DAUGHTER AND GRANDSON AND THROWS THEM INTO THE SEA?

Well, a fisherman rescued us. I grew up strong and handsome on the island of Seriphus.

To prove myself as a hero, I agreed to hunt down Medusa—a Gorgon monster with snakes for hair and eyes that could turn a man to stone if he looked directly into them!

That's a bit scarier than a big cow, don't you think?

The gods gave me a magic sword and reflective shield so I could defeat Medusa.

I crept into the monster's lair and, looking into the reflection in my shield instead of looking directly at her, I was able to chop off Medusa's head.

Then I used her head to defeat a cruel giant called Atlas, by turning him into stone.

To top it off, I saved a beautiful princess named Andromeda from being sacrificed to a terrible sea monster. After I defeated the giant sea monster in a fierce battle, I married Andromeda and ruled the kingdom. Everyone loved me!

And that is why I, Perseus, am clearly the GREATEST HERO OF . . .

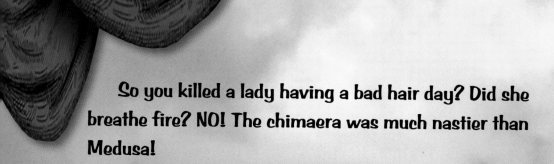

So you killed a lady having a bad hair day? Did she breathe fire? NO! The chimaera was much nastier than Medusa!

BE QUIET BELLEROPHON!

SHUSH BOTH OF YOU! JASON IS THE BEST!

THESEUS IS THE BRAVEST!

STOP RIGHT THERE ALL OF YOU! I am the narrator of this book and I am taking it back!

Which one of you completed his heroic tasks without any help from a god or princess or friend?

The flying horse I borrowed sure helped . . .

Medea's song was pretty useful . . .

Ariadne's ball of string came in handy . . .

That reflective shield was a good idea . . .

Just as I thought.

Kids, meet me in chapter 5.

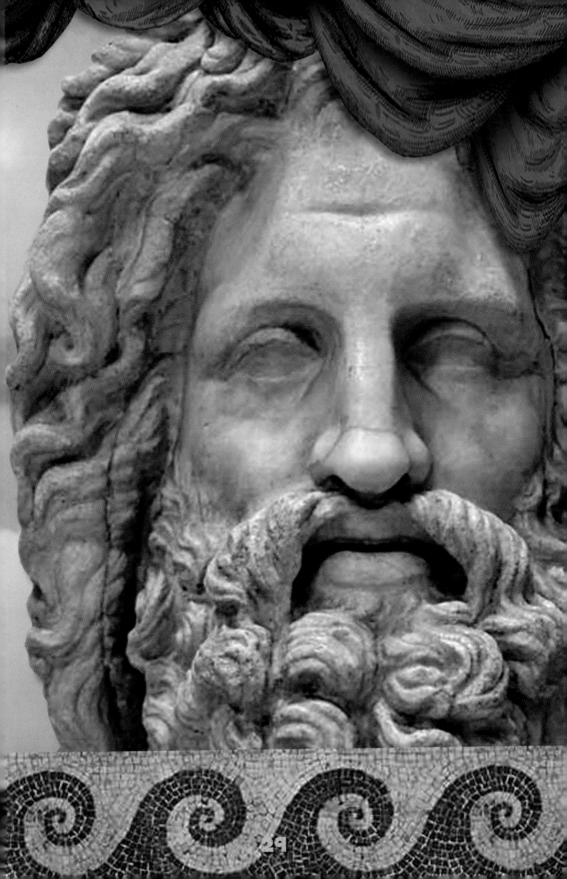

CHAPTER FIVE

GREEK HEROES ARE KIND OF JERKS

As you can see, like the Greek gods themselves, the heroes of ancient Greece, while very brave, were also sometimes not very nice. They broke promises, killed their own loved ones, and were sometimes selfish.

Let's just agree that there were many heroes in ancient Greece, all of whom did great deeds that live on thousands of years later in stories we love to share.

Books

Harris, John. *Greece! Rome! Monsters!* Los Angeles: Getty Publications, 2002.

McCaughrean, Geraldine. *Greek Gods and Goddesses*. New York: Margaret K. McElderry Books, 1998.

Oh, Cirro. *Greek and Roman Mythology, Volumes 1, 2, & 3*. Singapore: Youngjin Singapore Pte, Ltd., 2005.

Works Consulted

Bulfinch, Thomas. *Bulfinch's Mythology: The Age of Fable*. Mineola, New York:
Dover Publications, 2000.

Green, Roger Lancelyn. *Tales of Greek Heroes*. London: Penguin Books, 1958, 2002.

Hamilton, Edith. *Mythology*. New York: Warner Books, 1999.

McLean, Mollie, and Anne Wiseman. *Adventures of Greek Heroes*. New York: Houghton Mifflin, 1961, 1989.

Rouse, W.H.D. *Gods, Heroes, and Men of Ancient Greece*. New York: New American Library, 1957, 2001.

On the Internet

Ancient Greeks

www.bbc.co.uk/schools/primaryhistory/ancient_greeks/

Gods and Heroes Today

www.mythweb.com